SCHIRMER'S LIBRARY
OF MUSICAL CLASSICS

Vol. 1798

MORITZ MOSZKOWSKI

Op. 72

15 Études de Virtuosité

For the Piano

ISBN 978-0-7935-5202-3

G. SCHIRMER, Inc.

DISTRIBUTED BY

 HAL•LEONARD®
CORPORATION

7777 W. BLUEMOUND RD. P.O. BOX 13819 MILWAUKEE, WI 53213

Printed in the U.S.A. by G. Schirmer, Inc.

15 Études de Virtuosité

"Per Aspera"

No. 1
E Major

Moritz Moszkowski
Op. 72

Printed in the U.S.A. by G. Schirmer, Inc.

No. 2
G Minor

Allegro brillante

12

No. 3
G Major

Vivo e con fuoco

44449

14

44449

15

44449

No. 4
C Major

Allegro moderato

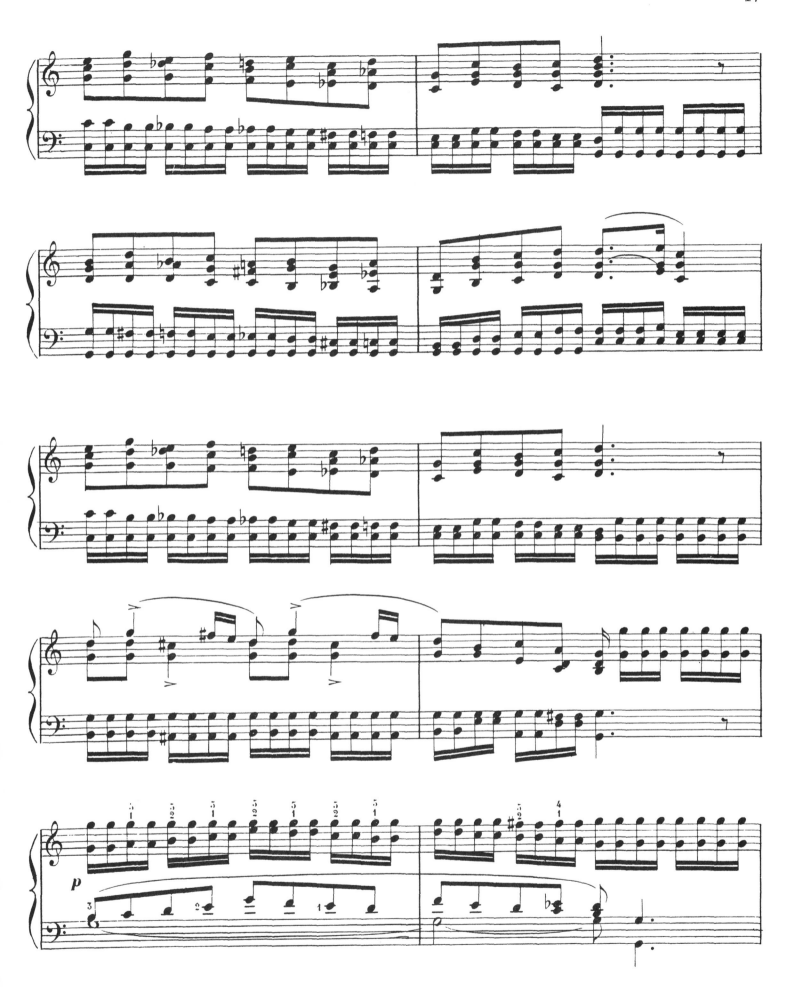

No. 5
C Major

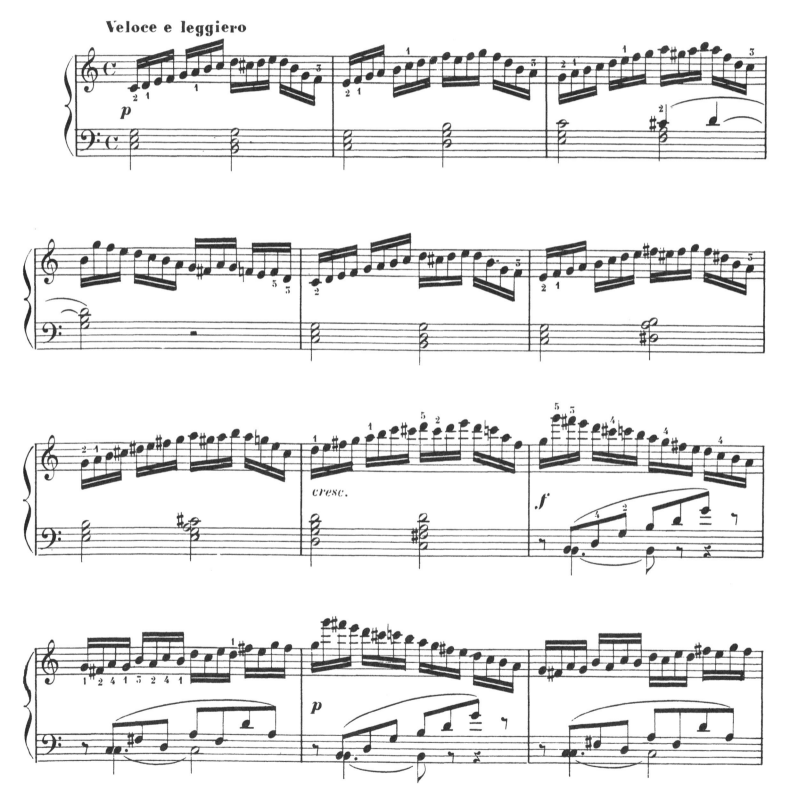

No. 6
F Major

No. 7
E♭ Major

Allegro energico

No. 8
C Major

No. 9
D Minor

No. 10
C Major

No. 11
A♭ Major

Presto e con leggierezza

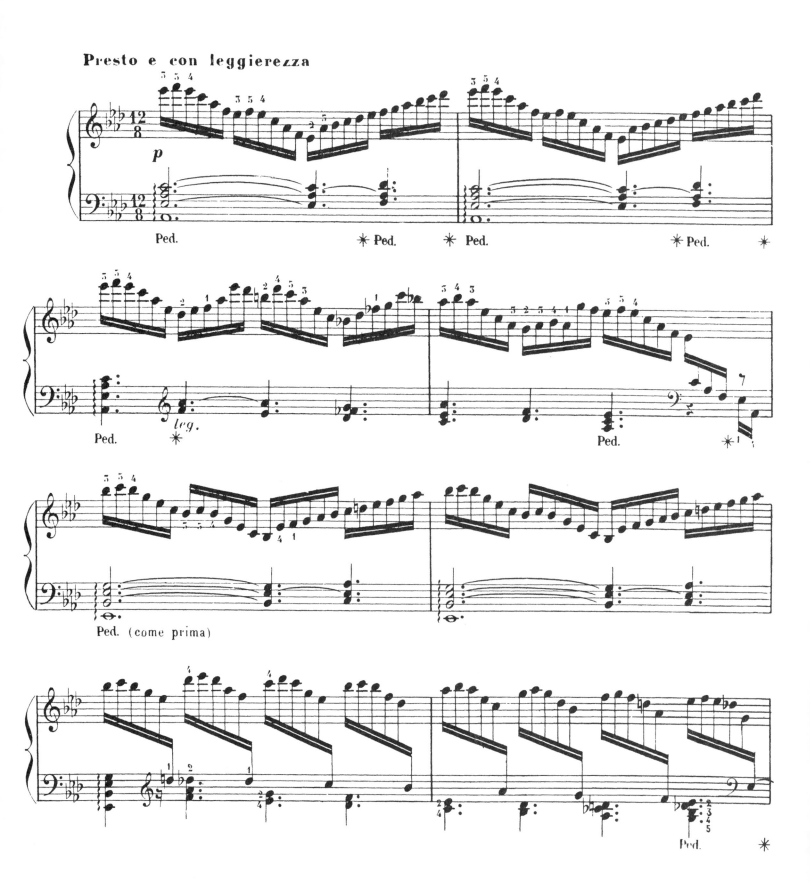

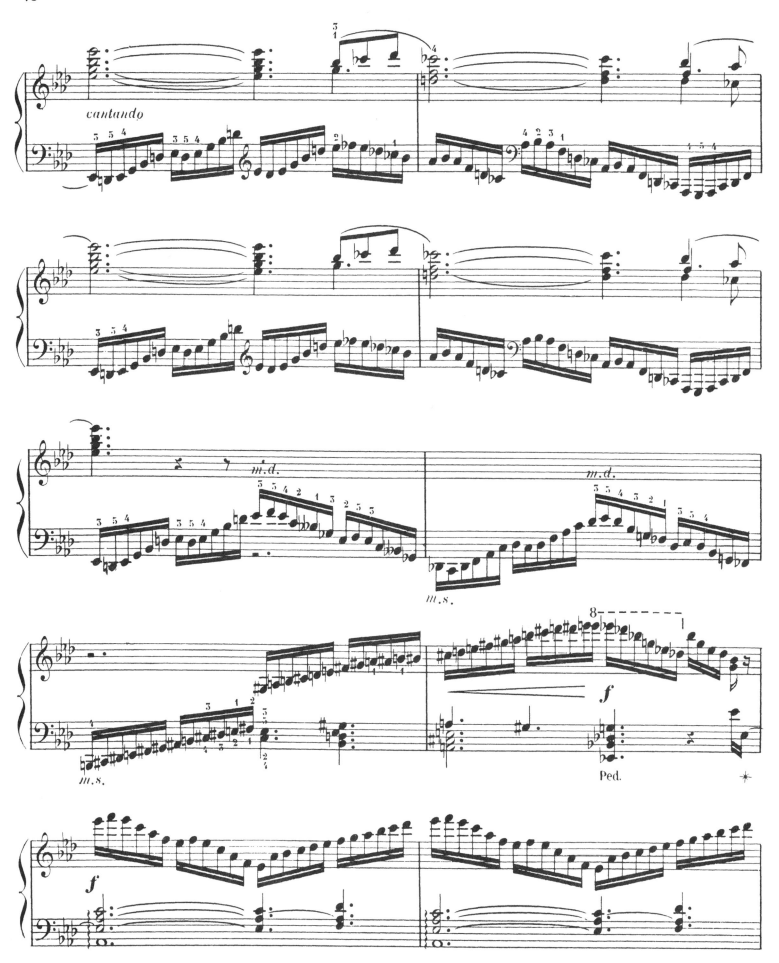

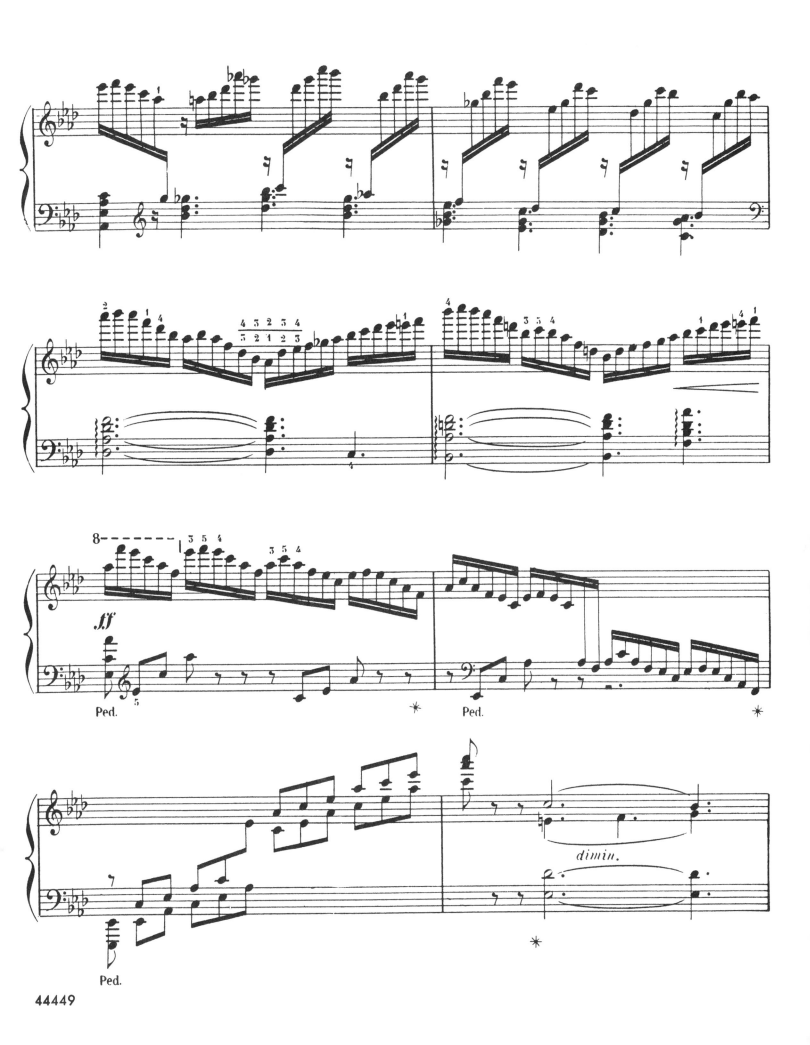

No. 12
Db Major

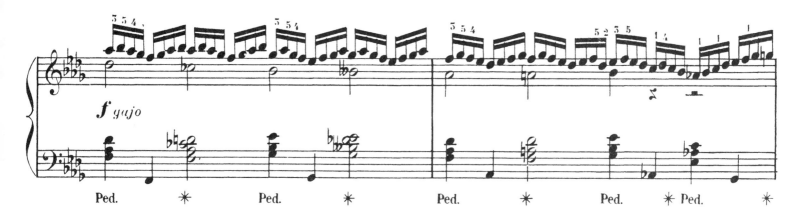

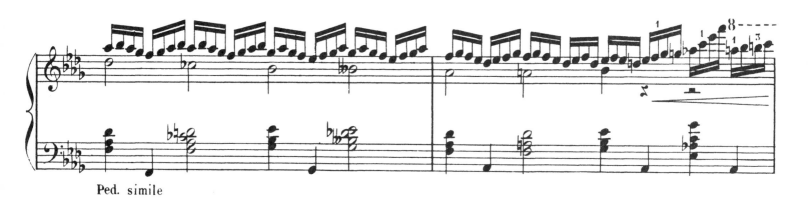

No. 13
A♭ Minor

Molto animato

p *con molta leggierezza*

con Ped.

44449

No. 14
C Minor

44449

No. 15
B Major

44449

44449